AF205594

Impressum
Verlag: BABADADA GmbH, Nedderfeld 112 , 22529 Hamburg
Geschäftsführer / Verlagsleitung: Harald Hof
Druck: Books on Demand GmbH, In de Tarpen 42, 22848 Norderstedt

Imprint
Publisher: BABADADA GmbH, Nedderfeld 112 , 22529 Hamburg, Germany
Managing Director / Publishing direction: Harald Hof
Print: Books on Demand GmbH, In de Tarpen 42, 22848 Norderstedt

school
escola

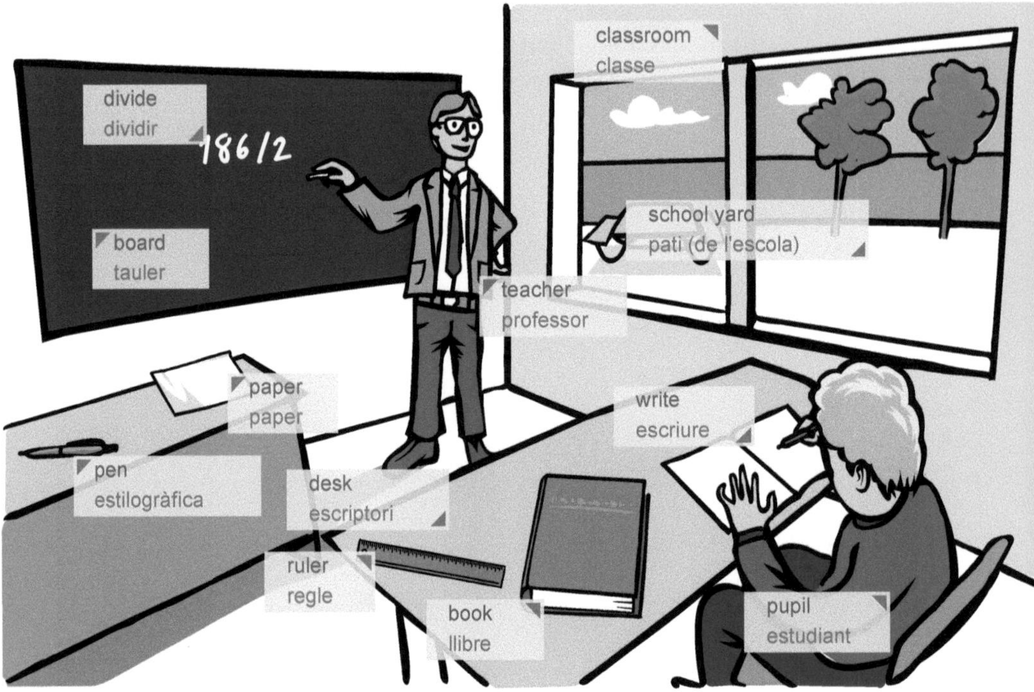
classroom
classe
divide
dividir
186/2
board
tauler
school yard
pati (de l'escola)
teacher
professor
paper
paper
write
escriure
pen
estilogràfica
desk
escriptori
ruler
regle
book
llibre
pupil
estudiant

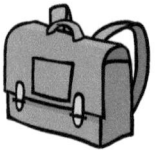

satchel

bossa

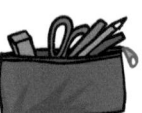

pencil case

estoig

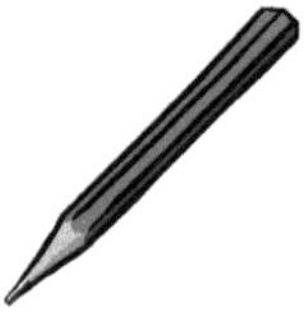

pencil

llapis

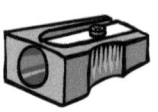

pencil sharpener

maquineta de fer punta

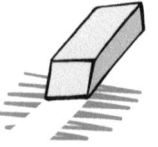

rubber

goma

drawing pad

bloc de dibuix

drawing	paintbrush	paint box
dibuix	pinzell	capsa de pintures

scissors	glue	exercise book
tisores	cola	quadern d'exercicis
	**12**	**2+2**
homework	number	add
deures	nombre	afegir
5-2	**2×2**	
subtract	multiply	calculate
sostreure	multiplicar	calcular
A	ABCDEFG HIJKLMN OPQRSTU VWXYZ	**hello**
letter	alphabet	word
lletra	alfabet	mot

text

text

read

llegir

chalk

guix

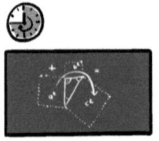

lesson

lliçó

register

llibre de classe

exam

examen

certificate

certificat

school uniform

uniforme escolar

education

formació

encyclopedia

enciclopèdia

university

universitat

microscope

microscopi

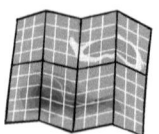

map

mapa

waste-paper basket

paperera

school - escola

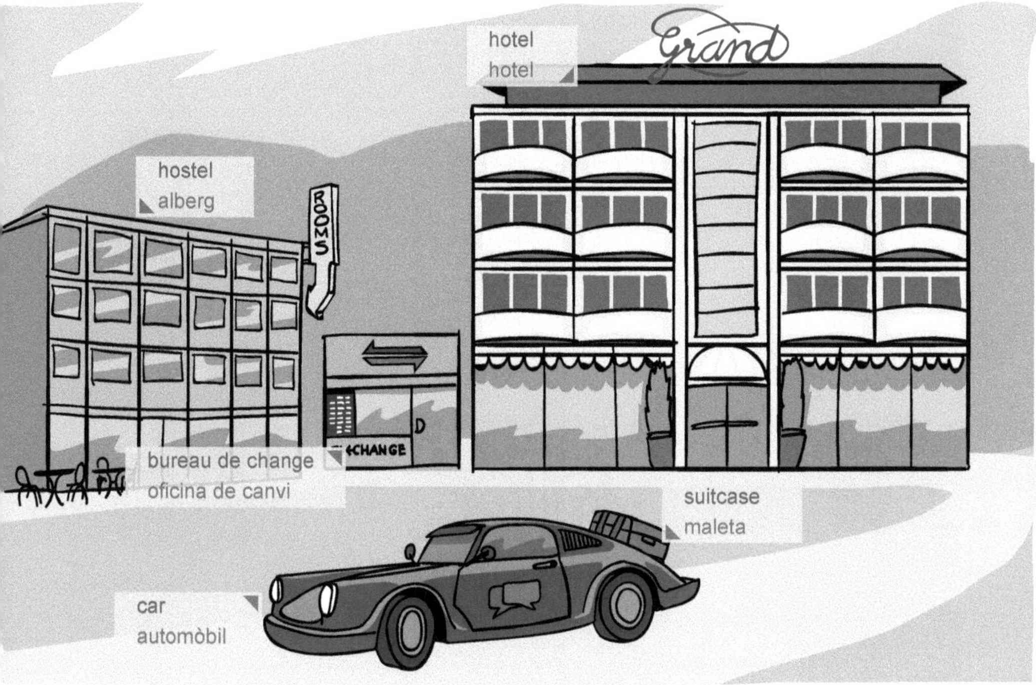
hotel
hotel
Grand
hostel
alberg
ROOMS
bureau de change
oficina de canvi
CHANGE
suitcase
maleta
car
automòbil

language
llengua

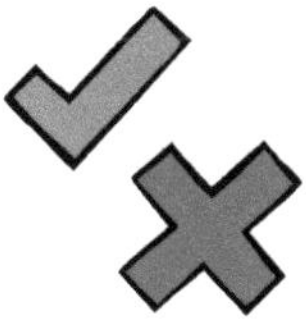

yes / no
sí / no

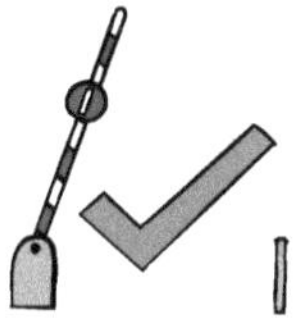

Okay
D'acord

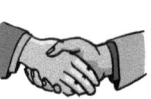

hello
Ey!

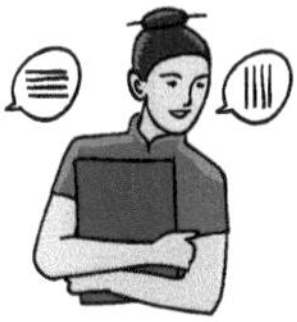

translator
traductora

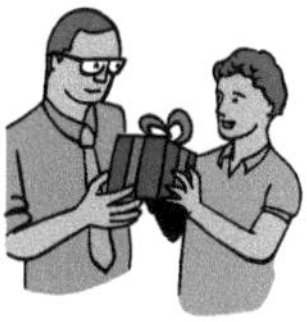

Thank you
gràcies

how much is…?

Quant costa… ?

I do not understand

No entenc

problem

problema

Good evening!

Bona nit!

Good morning!

bon dia!

Good night!

bona nit!

bye bye

fins aviat

direction

direcció

luggage

bagatge

bag

bossa

backpack

sarrona

guest

convidat

room

cambra

sleeping bag

sac de dormir

tent

tenda

tourist information

oficina de turisme

beach

platja

credit card

carta de crèdit

breakfast

esmorzar

lunch

dinar

dinner

sopar

ticket

bitllet

lift

ascensor

stamp

segell

border

frontera

customs

duana

embassy

ambaixada

visa

visat

passport

passaport

transport

transport

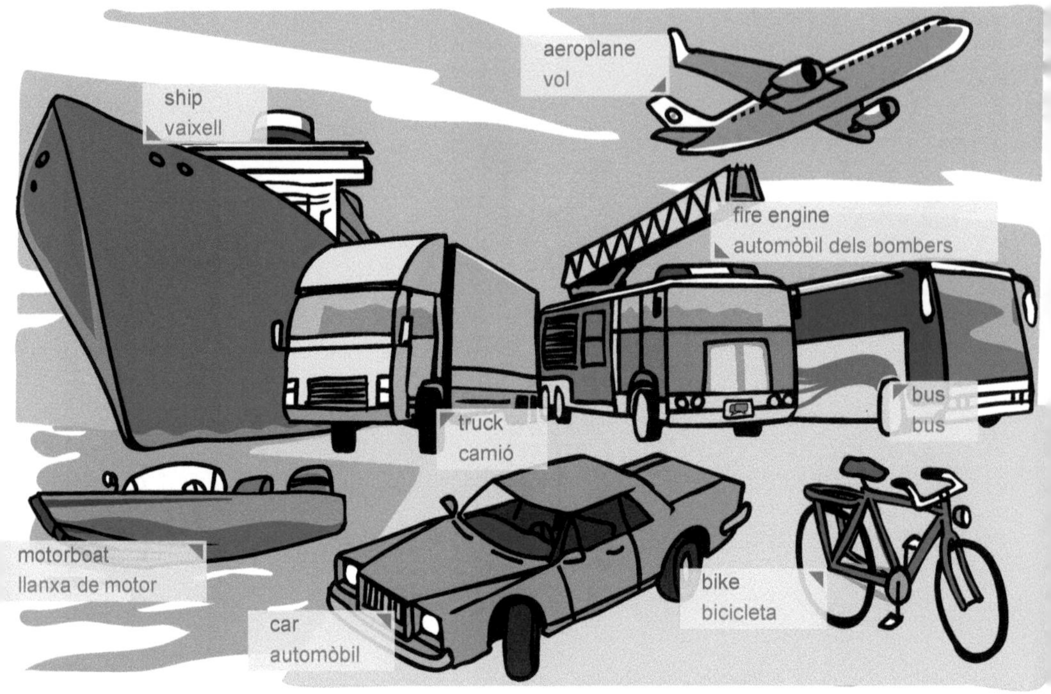

aeroplane
vol
ship
vaixell
fire engine
automòbil dels bombers
bus
bus
truck
camió
motorboat
llanxa de motor
bike
bicicleta
car
automòbil

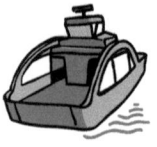

ferry

transbordador

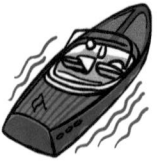

boat

barca

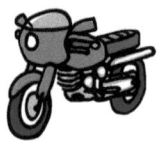

motorbike

moto

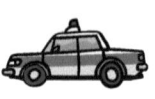

police car

automòbil de policia

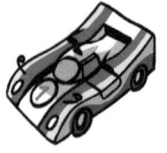

racing car

automòbil de curses

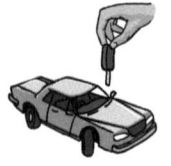

rental car

automòbil de lloguer

car sharing

vehicle compartit

breakdown truck

grua

refuse truck

camió de les escombraries

motor

motor

fuel

benzina

petrol station

benzineria

traffic sign

senyal de trànsit

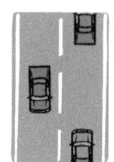

traffic

trànsit

traffic jam

embús

car park

aparcament

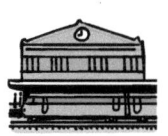

train station

estació de trens

tracks

vies

train

tren

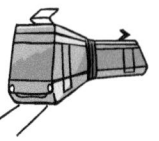

tram

tramvia

carriage

vagó

helicopter

helicòpter

airport

aeroport

tower

torre

passenger

passatger

container

contenidor

carton

capsa de cartó

cart

carretó

basket

cistella

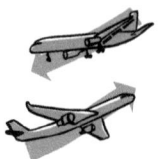

take off / land

enlairar-se / aterrar

city

ciutat

village

poble

city centre

centre de la ciutat

house

casa

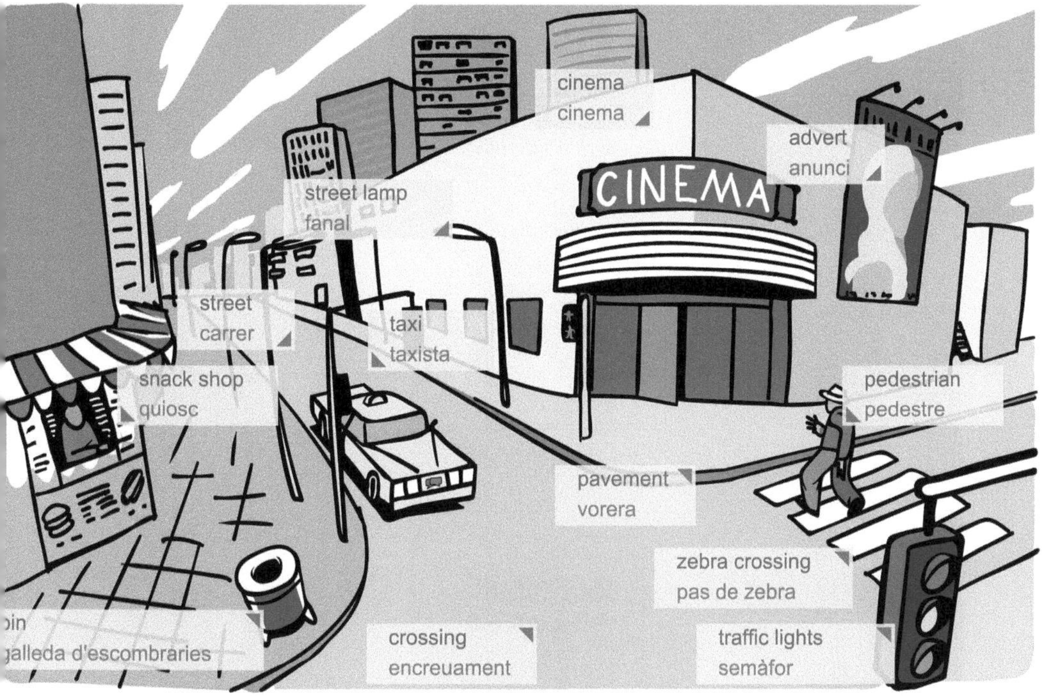
cinema
cinema
advert
anunci
street lamp
fanal
CINEMA
street
carrer
taxi
taxista
snack shop
quiosc
pedestrian
pedestre
pavement
vorera
zebra crossing
pas de zebra
in
alleda d'escombraries
crossing
encreuament
traffic lights
semàfor

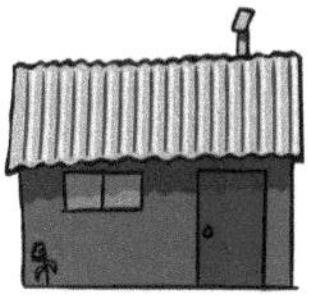

hut

cabana

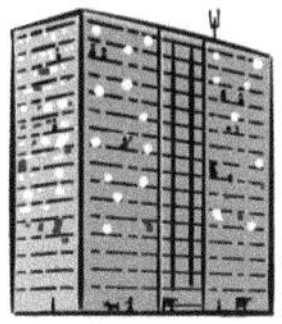

flat

apartament

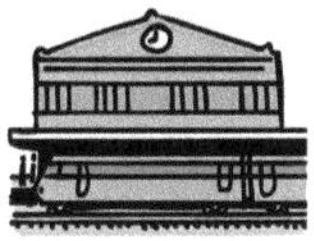

train station

estació de trens

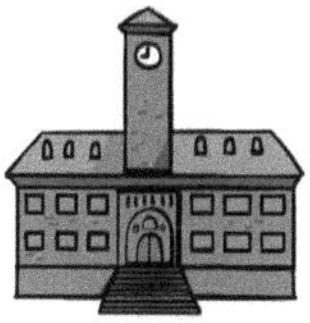

town hall

casa de la vila-ciutat

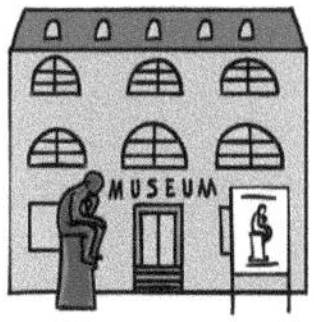

MUSEUM

museum

museu

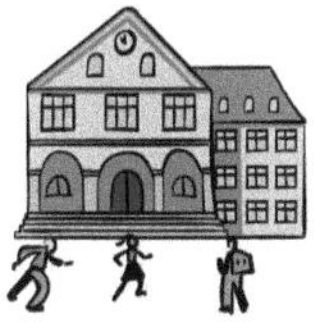

school

escola

university
universitat

bank
banca

hospital
hospital

hotel
hotel

pharmacy
farmàcia

office
oficina

book shop
llibreria

shop
botiga

florist's
floristeria

supermarket
supermercat

market
mercat

department store
gran magatzem

fishmonger's
peixateria

shopping centre
centre comercial

harbour
port

park

parc

bench

banc

bridge

pont

stairs

escala

underground

metro

tunnel

túnel

bus stop

parada d'autobús

bar

bar

restaurant

restaurant

postbox

bústia de correu

street sign

senyal indicador

parking meter

parquímetre

zoo

zoo

swimming pool

piscina

mosque

mesquita

farm

granja

pollution

pol·lució

graveyard

cementiri

church

església

playground

parc infantil

temple

temple

landscape

paisatge

leaf
fulla

signpost
cartell indicador

way
camí

meadow
prat

stone
pedra

hiker
excursionista

tree
arbre

river
riu

grass
gespa

flower
flor

valley
vall

hill
muntanya

lake
llac

forest
bosc

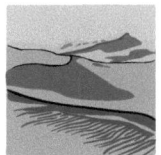

desert
desert

volcano
volcà

castle
castell

rainbow
arc de Sant Martí

mushroom
bolet

palm tree
palmera

mosquito
moscard

fly
mosca

ant
formiga

bee
abella

spider
aranya

landscape - paisatge

beetle

escarabat

frog

granota

squirrel

esquirol

hedgehog

eriçó

hare

llebre

owl

òliba

bird

ocell

swan

cigne

boar

senglar

deer

cervo

moose

ant

dam

presa

wind turbine

turbina

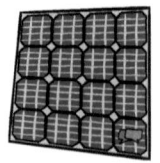

solar panel

panell solar

climate

clima

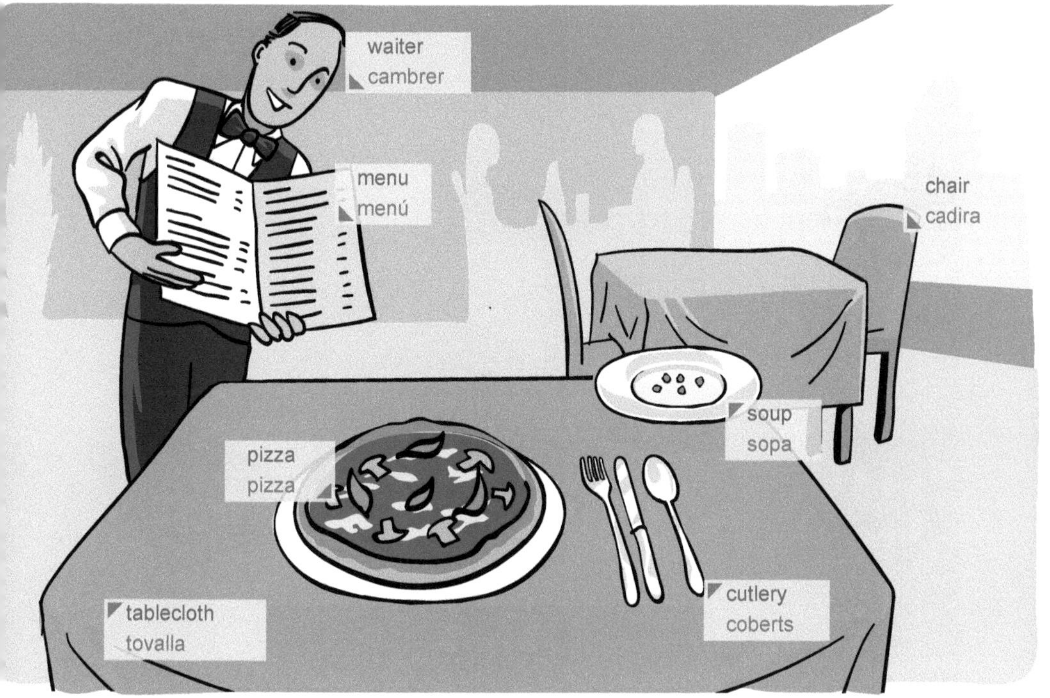

waiter
cambrer
menu
menú
chair
cadira
soup
sopa
pizza
pizza
cutlery
coberts
tablecloth
tovalla

starter
primer plat

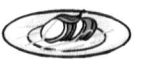

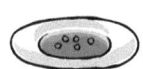

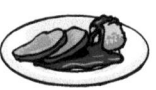

main course
plat principal

dessert
darreries

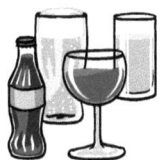

drinks
begudes

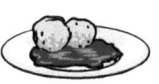

food
menjar

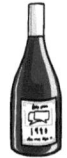

bottle
ampolla

fast food

menjar ràpid

street food

menjar de carrer

teapot

tetera

sugar bowl

sucrer

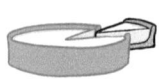

portion

porció

espresso machine

màquina d'espresso

high chair

trona

bill

factura

tray

plata

knife

ganivet

fork

forqueta

spoon

cullera

teaspoon

cullereta

serviette

tovalló

glass

got

restaurant - restaurant

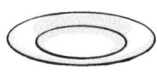

plate

plat

soup plate

plat de sopa

saucer

plateret

sauce

salsa

salt pot

saler

pepper mill

molinet de pebre

vinegar

vinagre

oil

oli

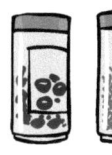

spices

espècies

ketchup

quètxup

mustard

mostassa

mayonnaise

maionesa

supermarket
supermercat

special offer
oferta especial
FOR
customer
client
dairy
productes lactis
trolley
carret de la compra
fruit
fruites

BUTCHERS

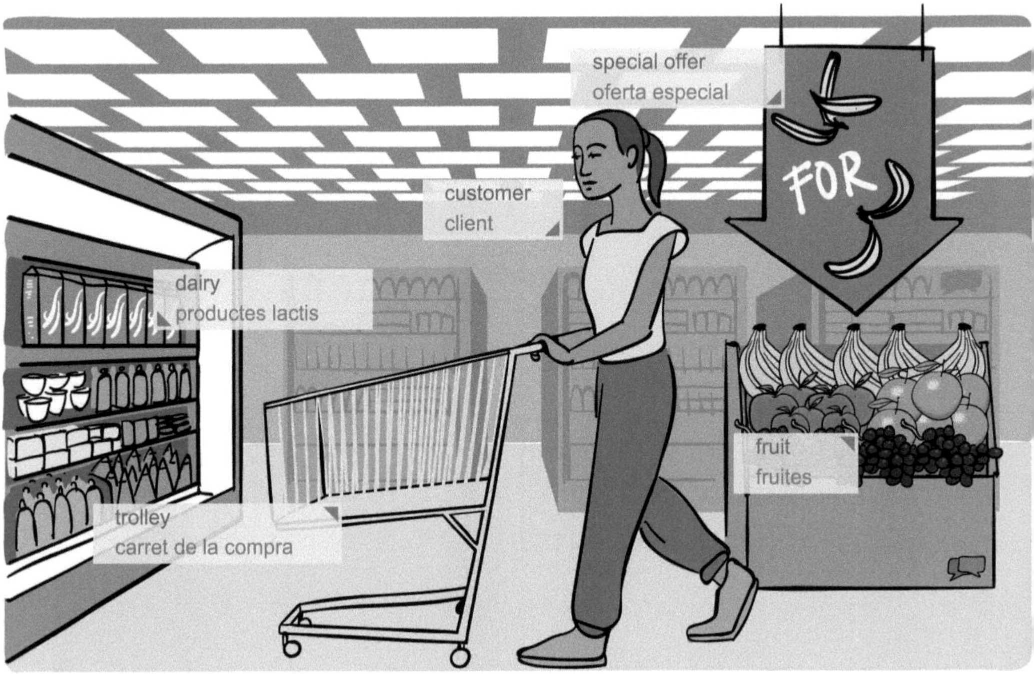

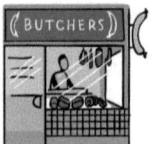

butcher´s

carnisseria

BAKERY

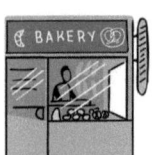

baker´s

forn de pa

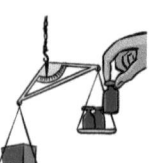

weigh

pesar

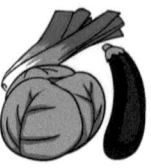

vegetables

verdures

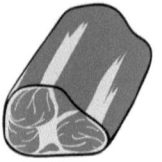

meat

carn

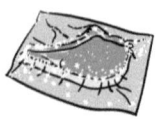

frozen food

menjar congelat

cold meat

carn freda

tinned food

conserves

washing powder

detergent en pols

sweets

dolços

household products

articles domèstics

cleaning products

productes de neteja

salesperson

venedora

till

caixa registradora

cashier

caixera

shopping list

llista de la compra

opening hours

horari d'obertura

wallet

portamonedes

credit card

carta de crèdit

bag

bossa

plastic bag

bossa de plàstic

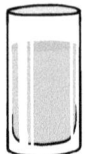

water

aigua

juice

suc

milk

llet

coke

coca-cola

wine

vi

beer

cervesa

alcohol

alcohol

cocoa

cacau

tea

te

coffee

cafè

espresso

espresso

cappuccino

cappuccino

banana

banana

apple

poma

orange

taronja

melon

síndria

lemon

llimona

carrot

pastanaga

garlic

all

bamboo

bambú

onion

ceba

mushroom

bolet

nuts

avellanes

noodles

fideus

spaghetti

espaguetis

rice

arròs

salad

amanida

chips

patates fregides

fried potatoes

patates fregides

pizza

pizza

hamburger

hamburguesa

sandwich

entrepà

cutlet

escalopa

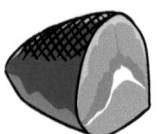

ham

cuixot

salami

salami

sausage

salsitxa

chicken

pollastre

roast

rostit

fish

peix

porridge oats

flocs de civada

muesli

musli

cornflakes

cereals

flour

farina

croissant

croissant

bread roll

panet

bread

pa

toast

torrada

biscuits

bescuits

butter

mantega

curd

mató

cake

pastís

egg

ou

fried egg

ou fregit

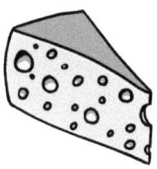

cheese

formatge

ice cream

gelat

sugar

sucre

honey

mel

jam

melmelada

chocolate spread

crema de xocolata

curry

curri

farm
granja

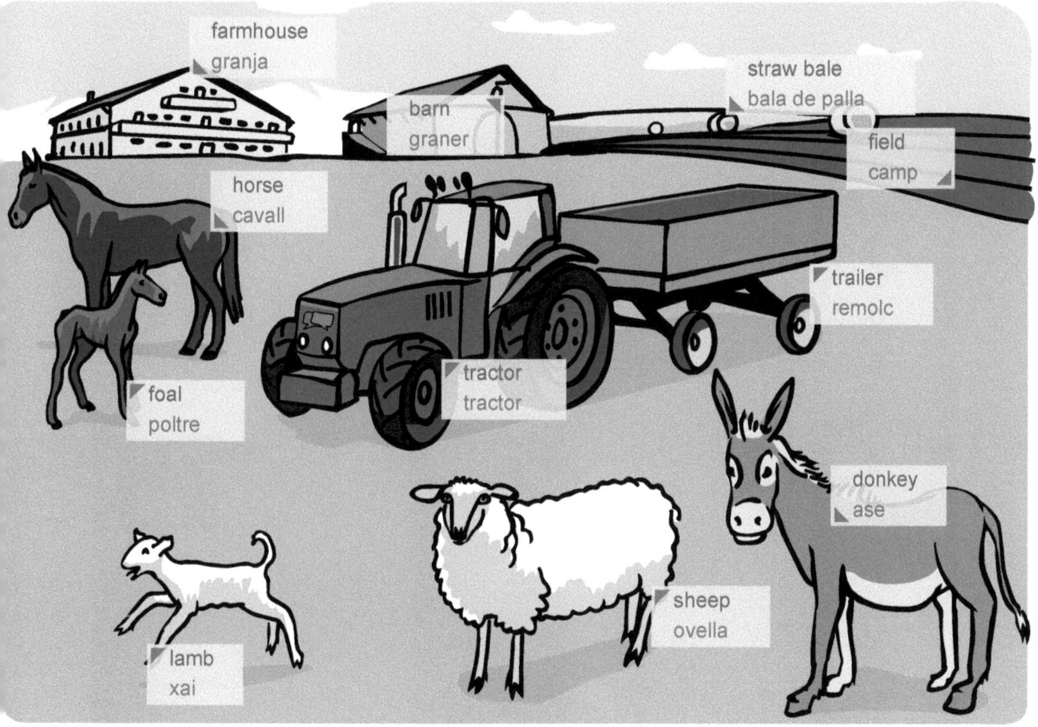
farmhouse
granja
barn
graner
straw bale
bala de palla
field
camp
horse
cavall
trailer
remolc
tractor
tractor
foal
poltre
donkey
ase
sheep
ovella
lamb
xai

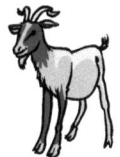

goat

cabra

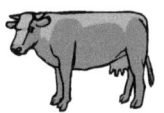

cow

vaca

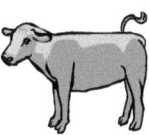

calf

vedella

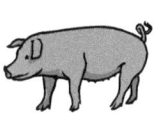

pig

porc

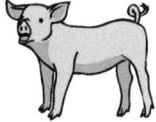

piglet

garrí

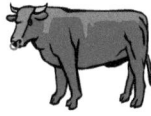

bull

bou

goose

oca

duck

ànec

chick

poll

hen

gall

cock

gallina

rat

rata

cat

gat

mouse

ratolí

ox

bou

dog

gos

doghouse

gossera

garden hose

mànega de regar

watering can

regadora

scythe

dalla

plough

arada

sickle

falç

hoe

aixada

pitchfork

forca

axe

destral

wheelbarrow

carretó

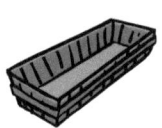

trough

abeurador

milk can

lletera

sack

sac

fence

tanca

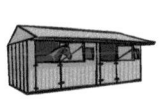

stable

establa

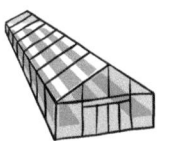

greenhouse

hivernacle

soil

sòl

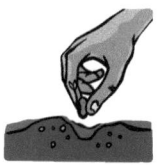

seed

llavor

fertilizer

adob

combine harvester

collidora

harvest

collir

harvest

collita

yams

nyam

wheat

blat

soy

soja

potato

patata

corn

blat de moro o d'indi

rapeseed

colza

fruit tree

arbre fruiter

cassava

mandioca

cereals

cereals

house
casa

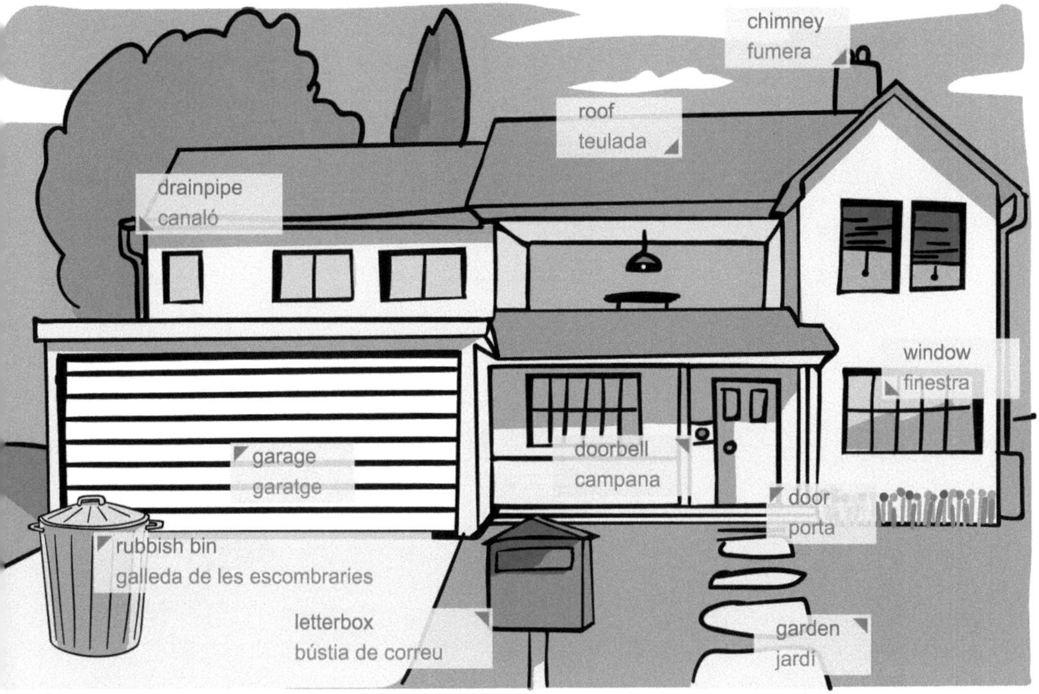
chimney
fumera
roof
teulada
drainpipe
canaló
window
finestra
garage
garatge
doorbell
campana
door
porta
rubbish bin
galleda de les escombraries
letterbox
bústia de correu
garden
jardí

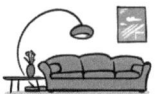

living room
sala d'estar

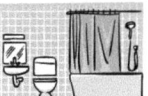

bathroom
bany

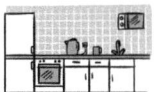

kitchen
cuina

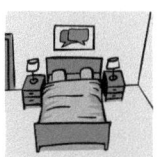

bedroom
cambra de dormir

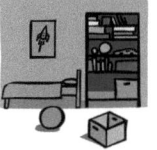

child's room
cambra de nen

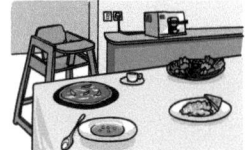

dining room
menjador

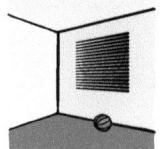

floor

sòl

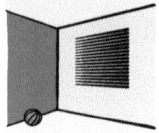

wall

paret

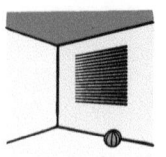

ceiling

sostre

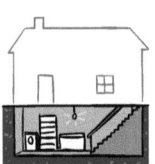

cellar

soterrani

sauna

sauna

balcony

balcó

terrace

terrassa

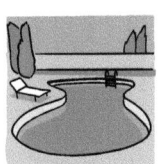

pool

piscina

lawn mower

tallagespa

sheet

vànova

bedspread

cobrellit

bed

llit

broom

escombra

bucket

galleda

switch

interruptor

living room
sala d'estar

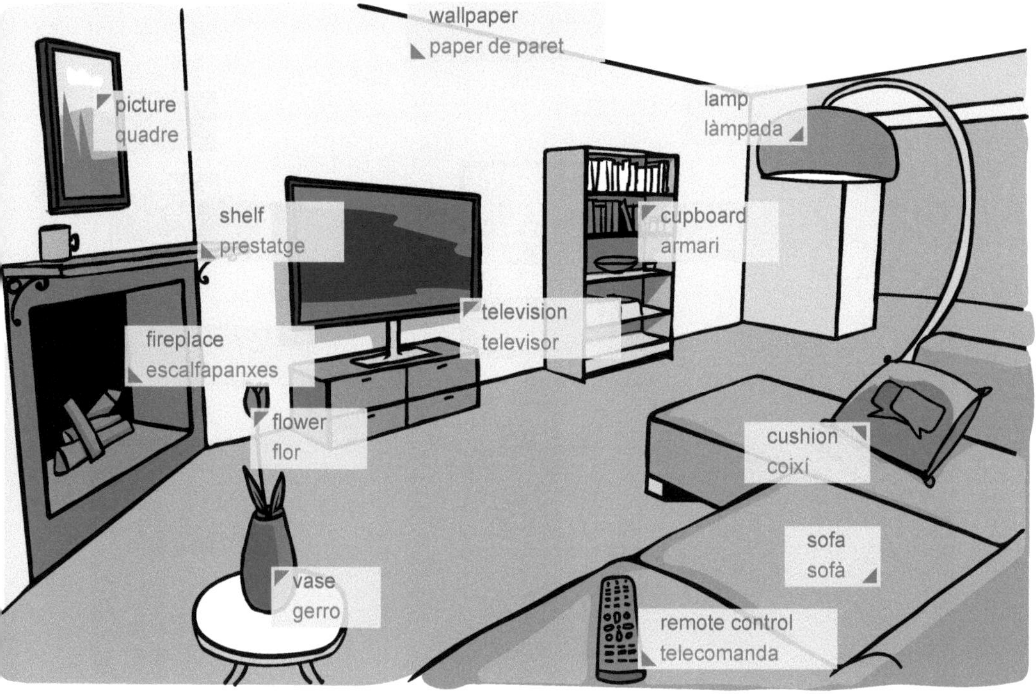
wallpaper
paper de paret
picture
quadre
lamp
làmpada
shelf
prestatge
cupboard
armari
television
televisor
fireplace
escalfapanxes
flower
flor
cushion
coixí
sofa
sofà
vase
gerro
remote control
telecomanda

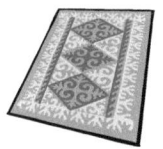

carpet

catifa

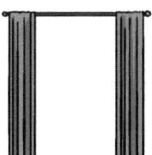

curtain

cortina

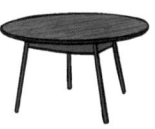

table

taula

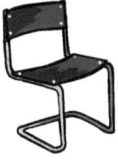

chair

cadira

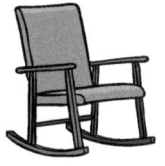

rocking chair

cadira gronxadora

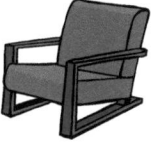

armchair

cadiral

book

llibre

blanket

llençol

decoration

decoració

firewood

llenya

film

film

hi-fi equipment

cadena de música

key

clau

newspaper

diari

painting

pintura

poster

cartell

radio

ràdio

notepad

bloc de notes

hoover

aspiradora

cactus

cactus

candle

candela

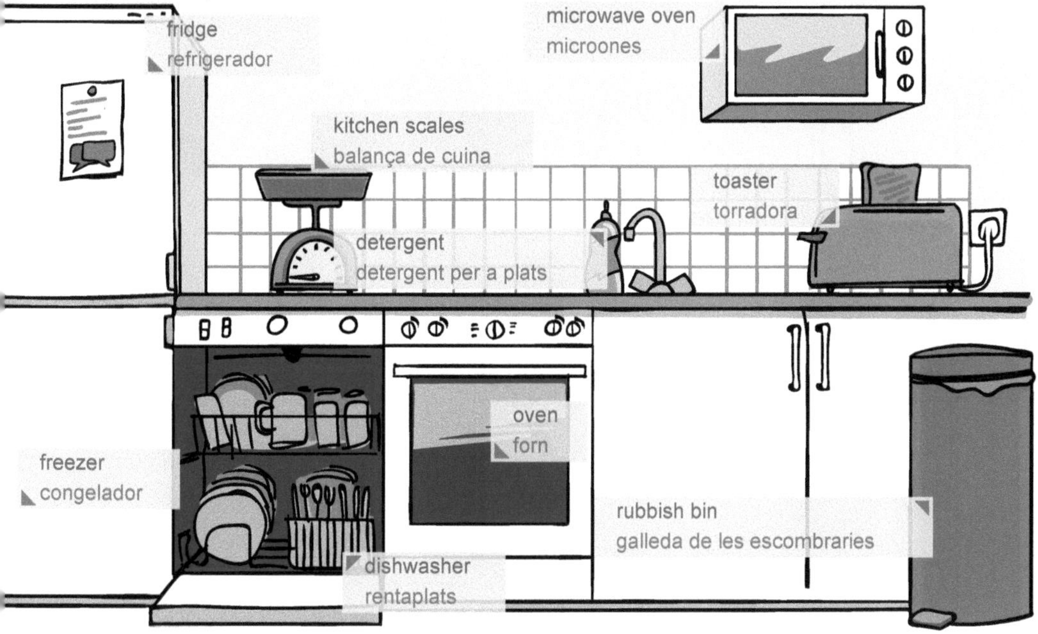

fridge
refrigerador

microwave oven
microones

kitchen scales
balança de cuina

toaster
torradora

detergent
detergent per a plats

freezer
congelador

oven
forn

rubbish bin
galleda de les escombraries

dishwasher
rentaplats

cooker

cuina de fogons

pot

olla

cast-iron pot

olla de ferro colat

wok / kadai

wok / karahi

pan

paella

kettle

bullidor

steamer

olla de vapor

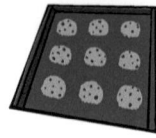

baking tray

plata de forn

crockery

vaixella

mug

tassa grossa

bowl

bol

chopsticks

bastonets xinesos

ladle

culler

spatula

espàtula

whisk

batedor

strainer

colador

sieve

sedàs

grater

ratllador

mortar

morter

barbecue

barbacoa

open fire

foc a terra

chopping board

taula de tallar

rolling pin

corró

corkscrew

llevataps

can

pot de conserva

can opener

obridor

pot holder

agafador

sink

aigüera

brush

raspall

sponge

esponja

blender

batedora

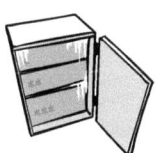

deep freezer

congelador

baby bottle

biberó

tap

aixeta

kitchen - cuina

bathroom
bany

heating
calefacció
towel
tovallola
shower
dutxa
shower curtain
cortina de dutxa
bubble bath
bany de bombolles
bathtub
banyera
glass
got
washing machine
rentadora
tiles
rajoles
tap
aixeta
potty
orinal
sink
aigüera

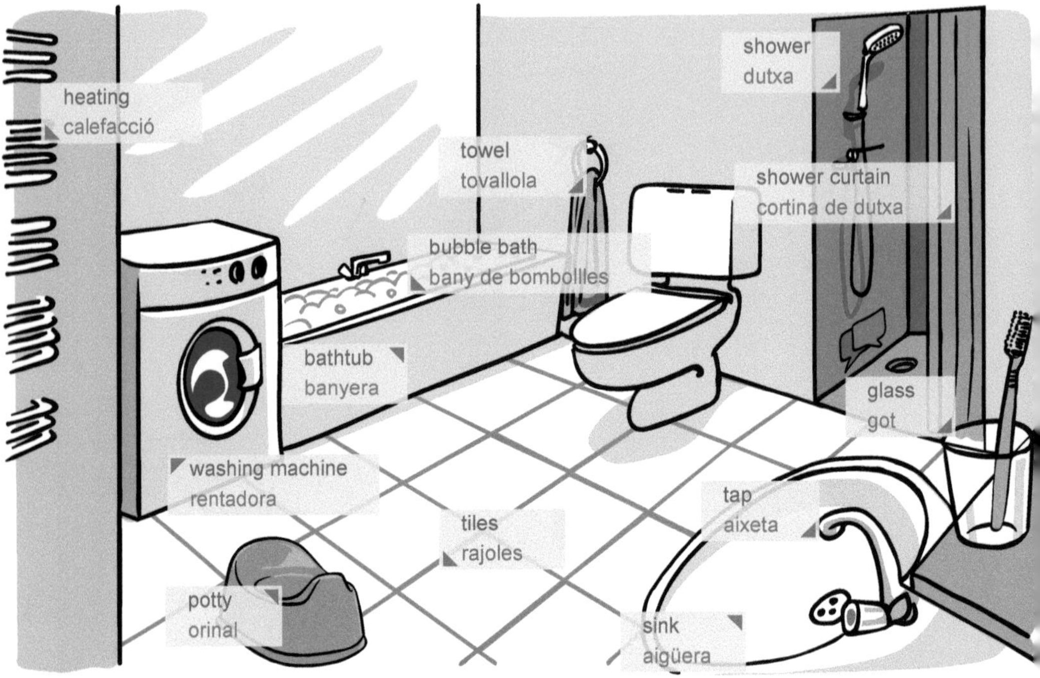

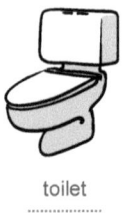

toilet
lavabo

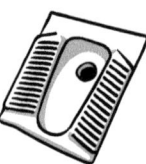

squat toilet
lavabo turc

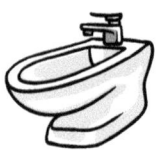

bidet
bidet

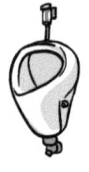

urinal
orinador

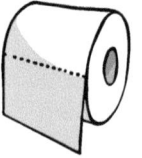

toilet paper
paper higiènic

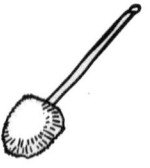

toilet brush
escombreta de sanitari

toothbrush

raspall de dents

toothpaste

pasta de dents

dental floss

fil dental

wash

rentar

handheld shower

pom de dutxa

douche

dutxa íntima

basin

rentamans

back brush

raspall per a l'esquena

soap

sabó

shower gel

gel de dutxa

shampoo

xampú

flannel

manyopla de bany

drain

bonera

cream

crema

deodorant

desodorant

mirror

mirall

hand mirror

mirall-espill de mà

razor

maquineta de rasar

shaving foam

espuma de barbejar

aftershave

loció post-rasada

comb

pinta

brush

raspall

hair dryer

eixugador

hairspray

laca

makeup

maquillatge

lipstick

pintallavis

nail varnish

esmalt d'ungles

cotton wool

cotó

nail scissors

tallaungles

perfume

perfum

washbag

estoig de bellesa

stool

tamboret

weighing scale

bàscula

bathrobe

barnús

rubber gloves

guants de goma

tampon

compresa higiènica

sanitary towel

compresa

chemical toilet

sanitari químic

child's room

cambra de nen

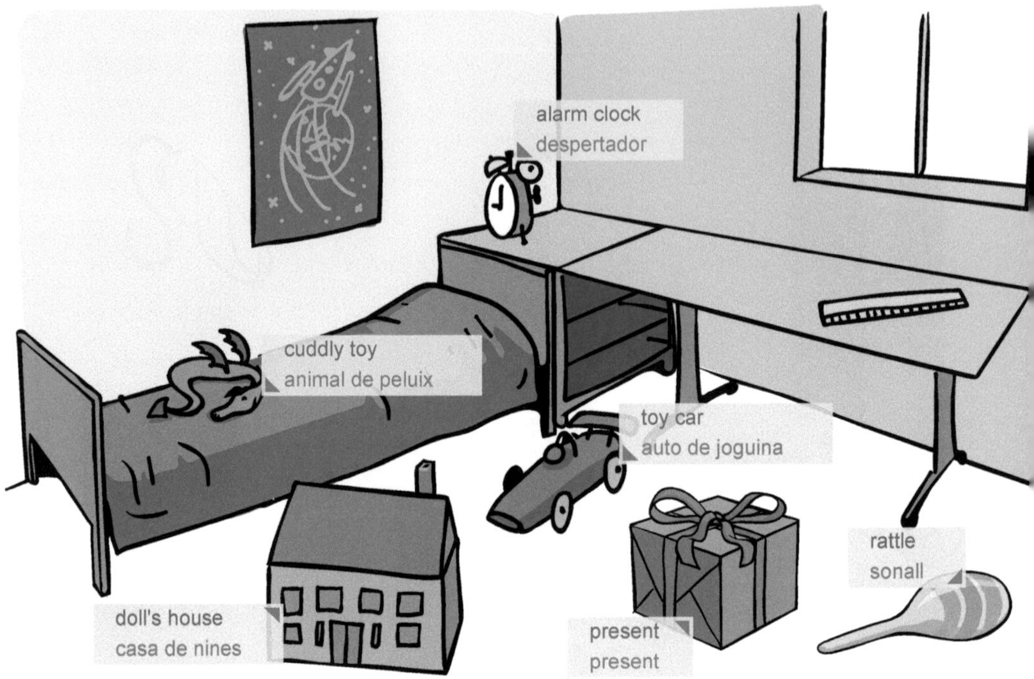
alarm clock
despertador
cuddly toy
animal de peluix
toy car
auto de joguina
rattle
sonall
doll's house
casa de nines
present
present

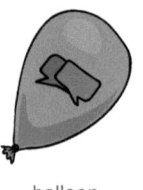

balloon

baló

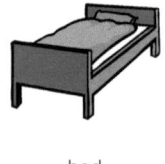

bed

llit

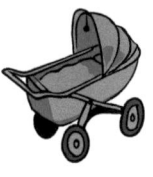

pram

cotxet per a nens

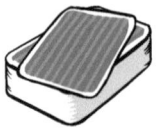

deck of cards

joc de cartes

jigsaw

trencaclosca

SUPER
MEGA

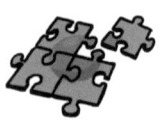

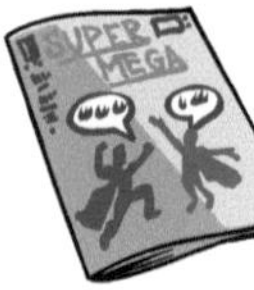

comic

historieta

lego bricks

peces de lego

building blocks

peces de construcció

action figure

ninot d'acció

babygrow

granota

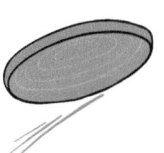

frisbee

frisbee

mobile

mòbil per a bressol

board game

joc de taula

dice

daus

model train set

tren elèctric

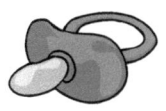

dummy

xumet

party

festa

picture book

llibre de dibuixos

ball

pilota

doll

nina

play

jugar

sandpit

sorrera

swing

gronxador

toys

joguines

video game console

consola de jocs de vídeo

tricycle

tricicle

teddy bear

osset de peluix

wardrobe

armari

clothing

roba

socks

mitjons

stockings

mitges

tights

mitja pantaló

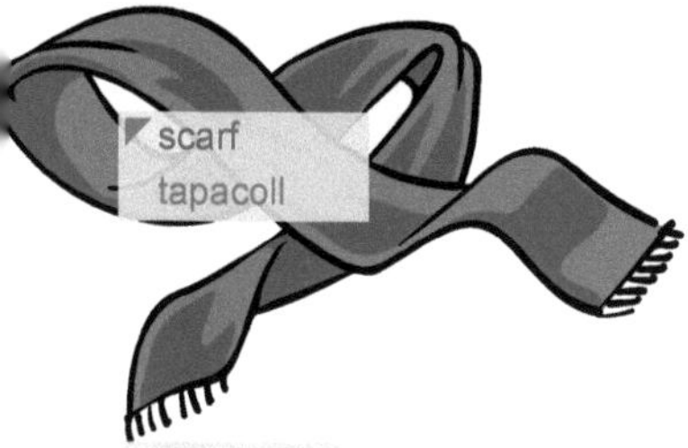

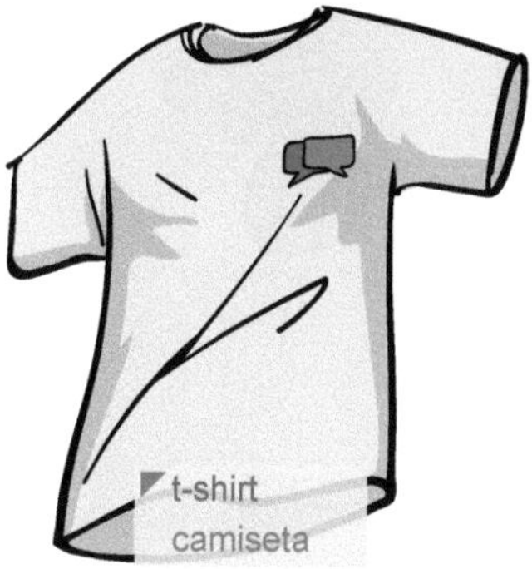

scarf
tapacoll

belt
cintura

umbrella
paraigua

t-shirt
camiseta

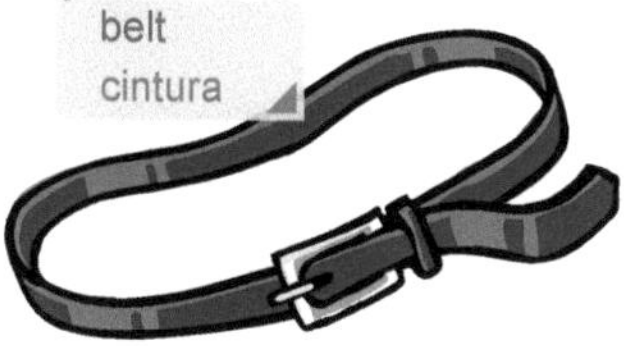

trainers
sabates d'esport

boots
botes

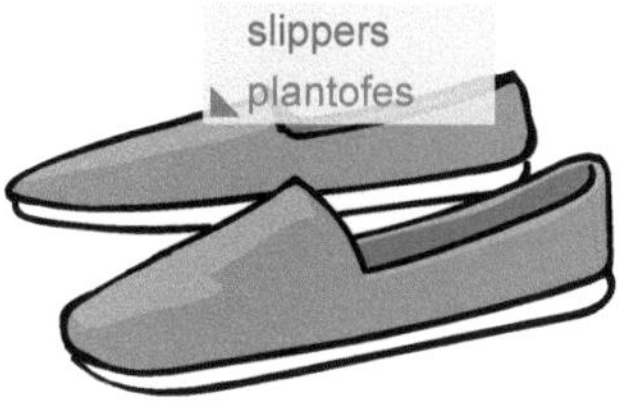

slippers
plantofes

sandals
....
sandàlies

shoes
....
sabates

rubber boots
....
botes de goma

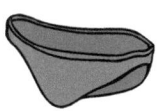

underpants
....
calçonets

bra
....
sostenidor

vest
....
guardapits

body

jjustacòs

trousers

pantalons

jeans

jeans

skirt

faldeta

blouse

brusa

shirt

camisa

pullover

jersei

hoodie

dessuadora

blazer

blazer

jacket

jaqueta

coat

mantell

raincoat

impermeable

costume

vestit de dona

dress

vestit de dona

wedding dress

vestit de núvia

suit

vestit d'home

nightgown

camisa de dormir

pyjamas

pijama

sari

sari

headscarf

mocador de cap

turban

turbant

burqa

burca

kaftan

caftan

abaya

abaia

swimsuit

vestit de bany

trunks

calçon(et)s de bany

shorts

pantalons curts

tracksuit

xandall

apron

davantal

gloves

guants

button

botó

glasses

ulleres

bracelet

braçalet

necklace

collaret

ring

anell

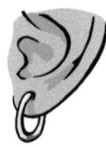

earring

orellera

cap

casquet

coat hanger

penjador

hat

capell

tie

corbata

zip

cremallera

helmet

casc

braces

elàstics

school uniform

uniforme escolar

uniform

uniforme

bib
pitet

dummy
xumet

nappy
bolquer

office
oficina

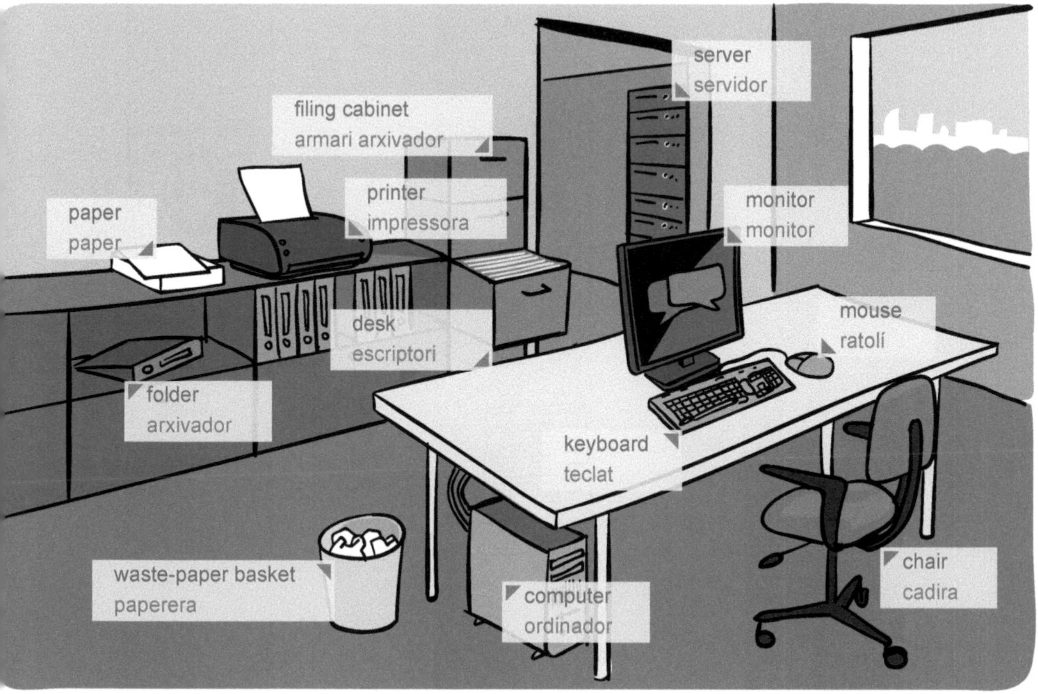

server
servidor

filing cabinet
armari arxivador

printer
impressora

monitor
monitor

paper
paper

mouse
ratolí

desk
escriptori

folder
arxivador

keyboard
teclat

chair
cadira

waste-paper basket
paperera

computer
ordinador

coffee mug
tassa de cafè

calculator
calculadora

internet
Internet

laptop

ordinador portàtil

letter

lletra

message

missatge

mobile

mòbil

network

xarxa

photocopier

fotocopiadora

software

programari

telephone

telèfon

plug socket

presa de corrent

fax machine

fax

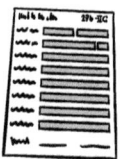

form

formulari

document

document

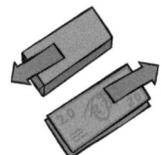

buy

comprar

pay

pagar

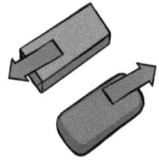

trade

comerciar

money

diners

dollar

dòlar

euro

euro

yen

ien

rouble

ruble

Swiss franc

franc suís

renminbi yuan

renminbi

rupee

rupia

cashpoint

caixa automàtica

bureau de change

oficina de canvi

gold

or

silver

argent

oil

petroli

energy

energia

price

preu

contract

contracte

tax

impost

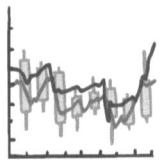

stock

acció

work

treballar

employee

treballador

employer

empresari

factory

fàbrica

shop

botiga

police officer
oficial de policia

fireman
bomber

cook
cuiner

doctor
doctora

pilot
pilot

gardener

jardiner

carpenter

fuster

seamstress

costurera

judge

jutge

chemist

química

actor

actor

bus driver

conductor d'autobús

taxi driver

taxista

fisherman

pescador

cleaning lady

dona de la neteja

roofer

ensostrador

waiter

cambrer

hunter

caçador

painter

pintor

baker

forner

electrician

electricista

builder

obrer de la construcció

engineer

enginyer

butcher

carnisser

plumber

llanterner

postman

correu

soldier

soldat

architect

arquitecte

cashier

caixera

florist

florista

hairdresser

perruquer

conductor

revisor

mechanic

mecànic

captain

capità

dentist

dentista

scientist

científic

rabbi

rabí

imam

imam

monk

monjo

clergyman

capellà

tools
eines

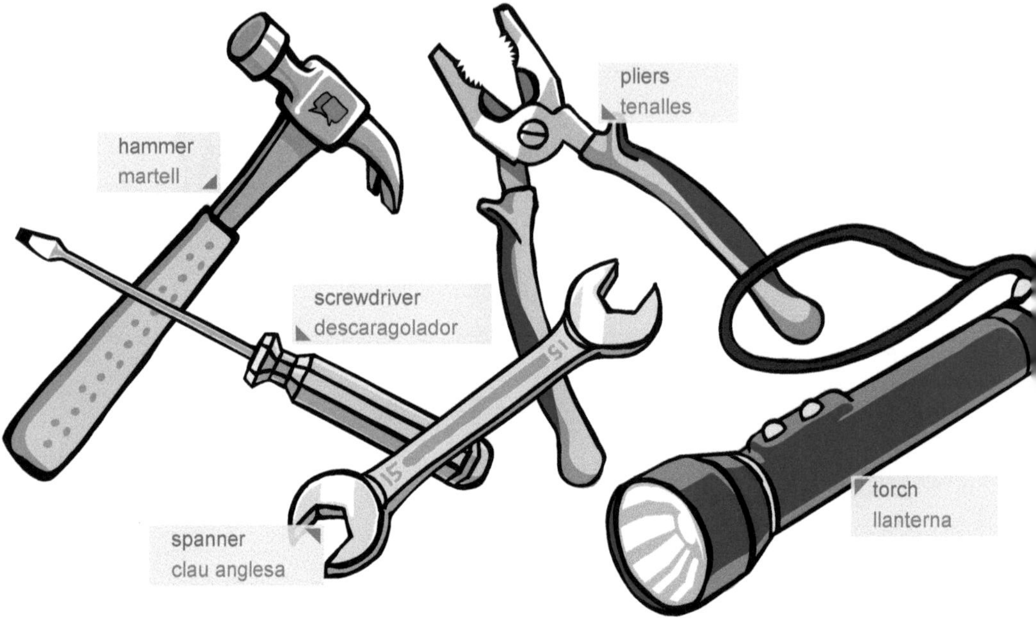
hammer
martell
pliers
tenalles
screwdriver
descaragolador
spanner
clau anglesa
torch
llanterna

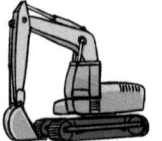

digger

excavadora

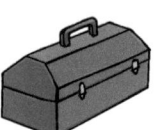

toolbox

caixa d'eines

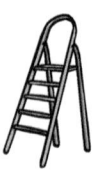

ladder

escala

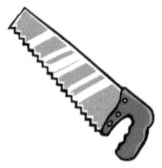

saw

serra

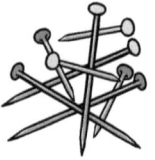

nails

claus

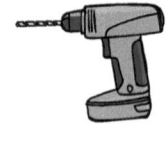

drill

trepant

repair

reparar

shovel

pala

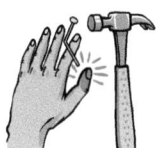

Damn!

Maleït siga!

dustpan

pala

paint pot

pot de pintura

screws

caragols

musical instruments

instrument de música

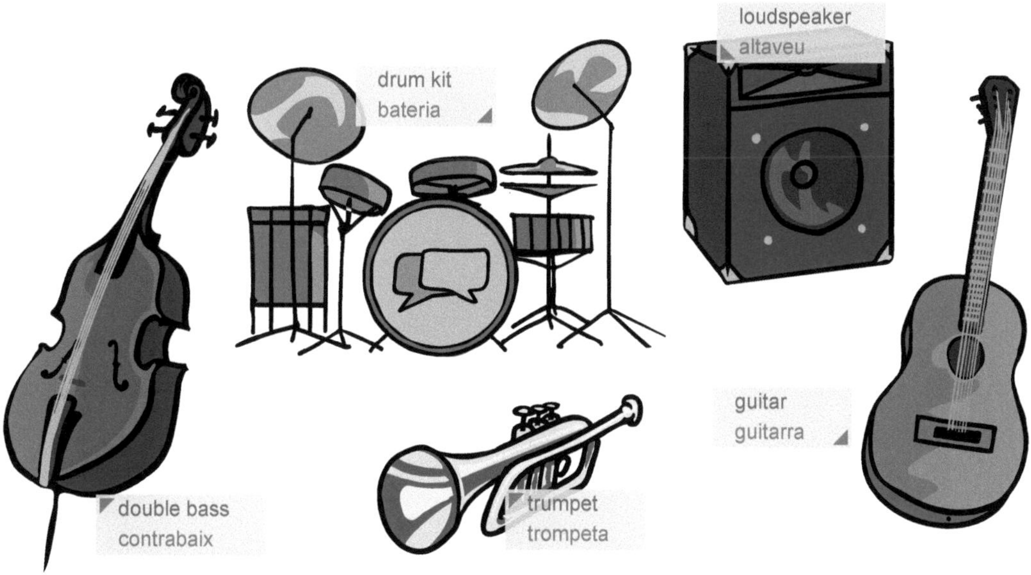

loudspeaker
altaveu

drum kit
bateria

guitar
guitarra

double bass
contrabaix

trumpet
trompeta

piano

piano

violin

violí

bass

baix

timpani

timbal

drums

tambor

keyboard

teclat

saxophone

saxofon

flute

flauta

microphone

micròfon

ZOO

ZOO

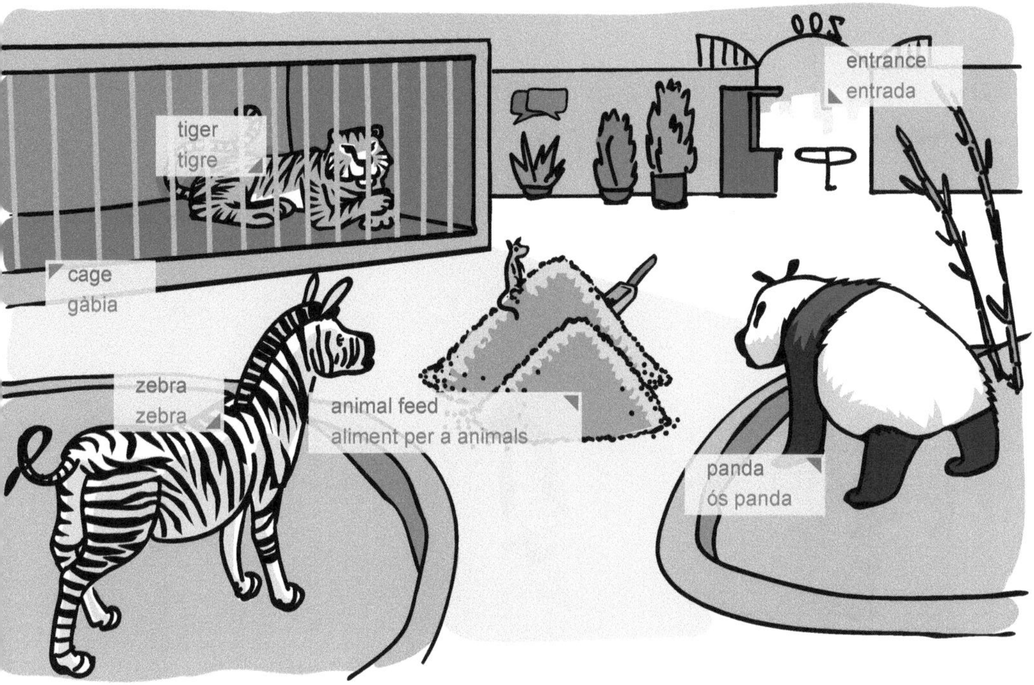
entrance
entrada
tiger
tigre
cage
gàbia
zebra
zebra
animal feed
aliment per a animals
panda
ós panda

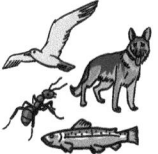

animals

animals

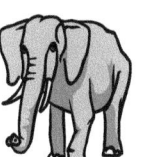

elephant

elefant

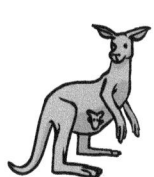

kangaroo

cangurú

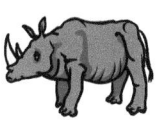

rhino

rinoceront

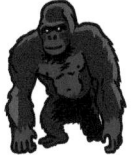

gorilla

goril·la

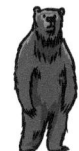

bear

ós

camel

camell

ostrich

estruç

lion

lleó

monkey

simi

flamingo

flamenc

parrot

papagai

polar bear

ós polar

penguin

pingüí

shark

ca mari

peacock

paó

snake

serp

crocodile

cocodril

zookeeper

guardià del zoo

seal

foca

jaguar

jaguar

pony

poni

leopard

lleopard

hippo

hipopòtam

giraffe

girafa

eagle

àliga

boar

senglar

fish

peix

turtle

tortuga

walrus

morsa

fox

guineu

gazelle

gasela

American football
futbol americà

cycling
ciclisme

tennis
tenis

basketball
bàsquet

swimming
natació

boxing
boxa

ice hockey
hoquei sobre gel

football
·················
futbol americà

badminton
·················
bàdminton

athletics
·················
atletisme

handball
·················
handbol

skiing
·················
esquí

polo
·················
polo

activities
activitats

laugh
riure
jump
saltar
hug
abraçar
walk
anar
sing
cantar
dream
somiar
pray
pregar
kiss
fer un petó

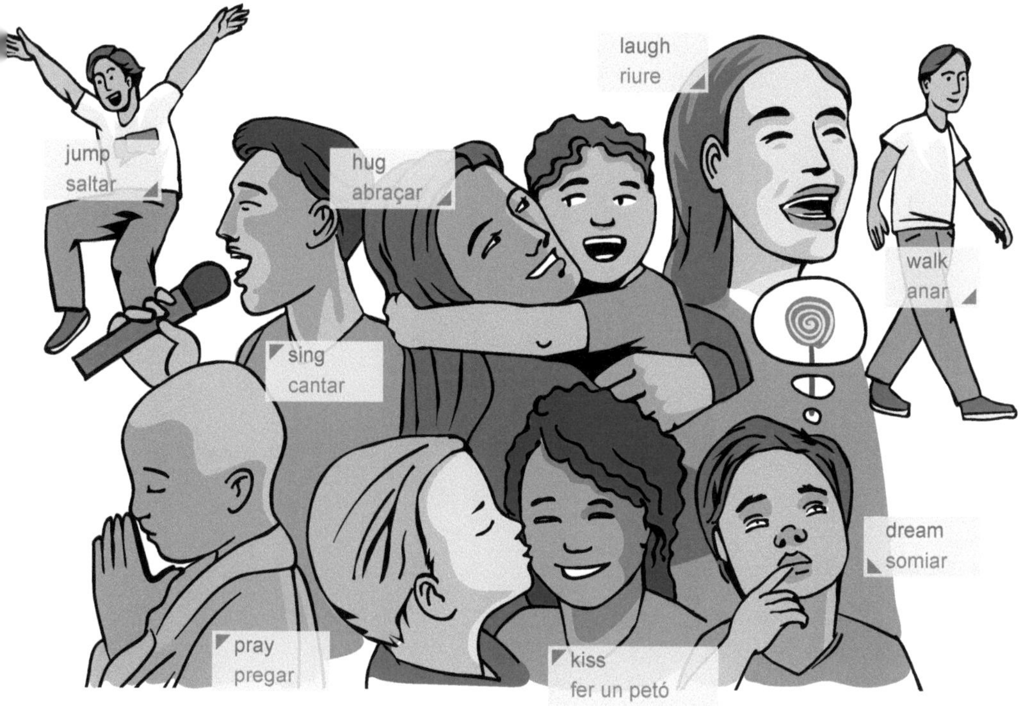

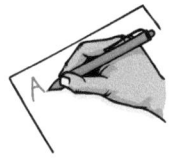

write
escriure

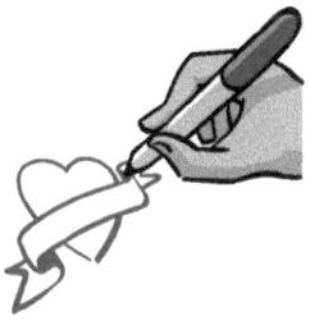

draw
dibuixar

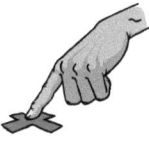

show
mostrar

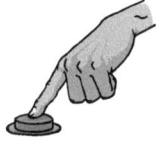

push
pitjar

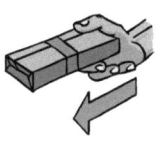

give
donar

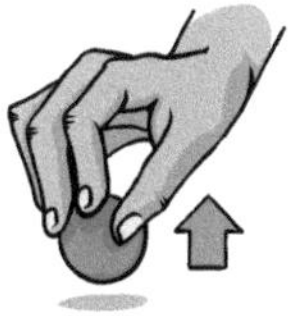

take
prendre

have
tenir

do
fer

be
ésser

stand
estar dret

run
córrer

pull
estirar

throw
llançar

fall
caure

lie
jeure

wait
esperar

carry
portar

sit
asseure's

get dressed
vestir-se

sleep
dormir

wake up
despertar-se

look at

mirar

cry

plorar

stroke

amoixar

comb

pentinar

talk

parlar

understand

comprendre

ask

demanar

listen

escoltar

drink

beure

eat

menjar

tidy up

endreçar

love

estimar

cook

cuinar

drive

conduir

fly

volar

activities - activitats

sail

navegar

calculate

calcular

read

llegir

learn

aprendre

work

treballar

marry

casar-se

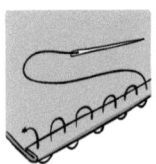

sew

cosir

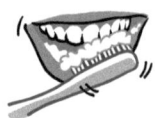

brush teeth

raspallar-se les dents

kill

matar

smoke

fumar

send

enviar

grandmother
àvia

grandfather
avi

father
pare

mother
mare

baby
nadó

daughter
filla

son
fill

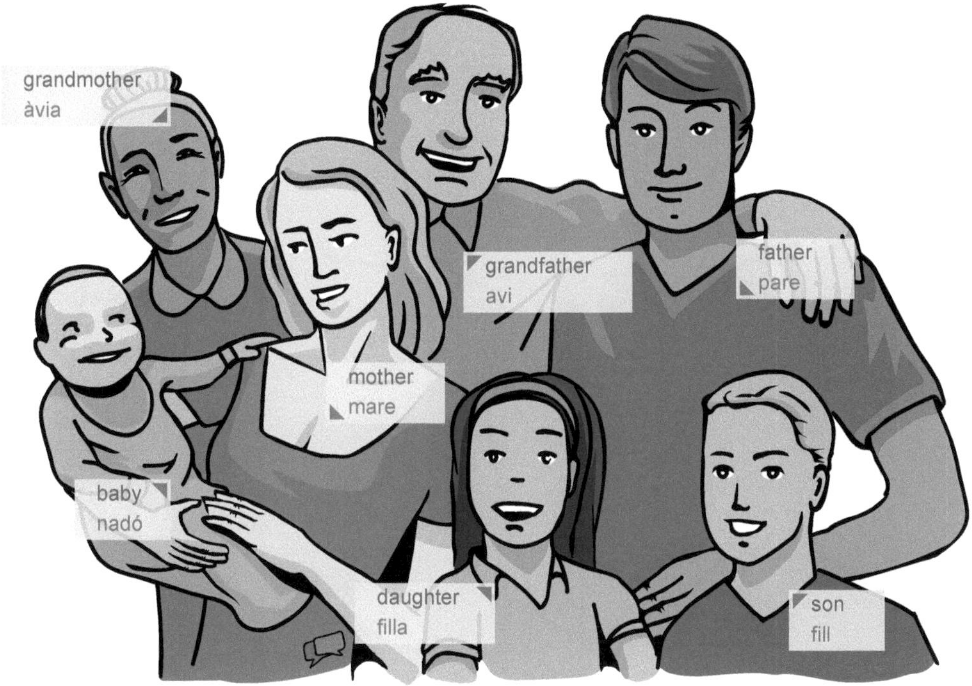

guest

convidat

aunt

tia

uncle

oncle

brother

germà

sister

germana

body

cos

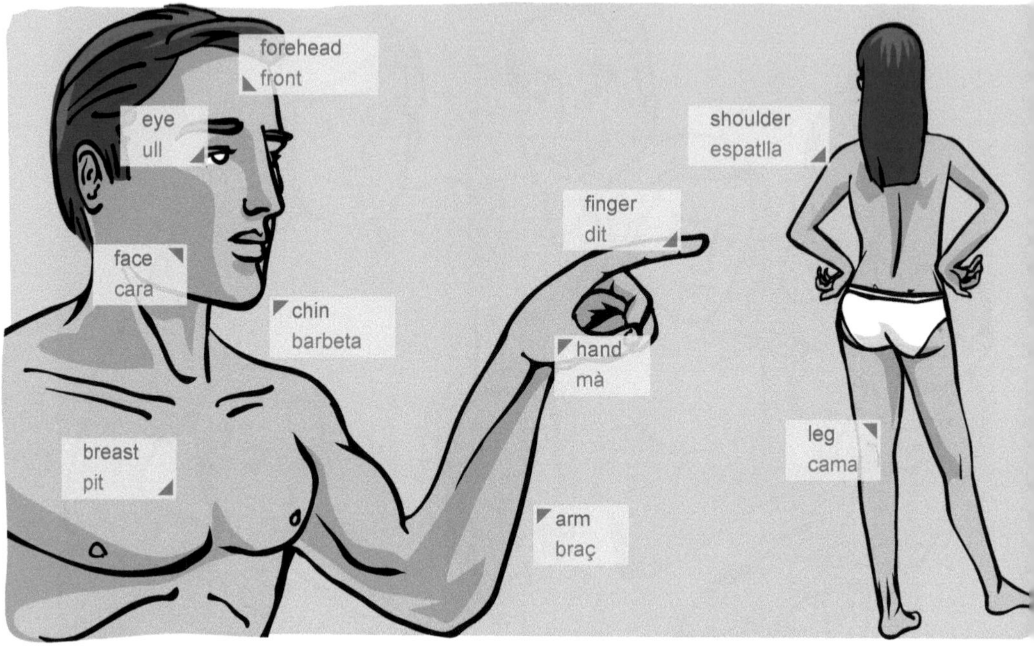

forehead
front

eye
ull

shoulder
espatlla

face
cara

finger
dit

chin
barbeta

hand
mà

breast
pit

leg
cama

arm
braç

baby
nadó

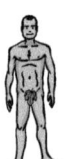

man
home

woman
dona

girl
noia

boy
noi

head
cap

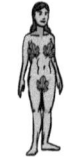

68   body - cos

back

esquena

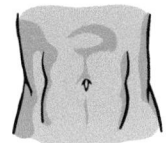

belly

panxa

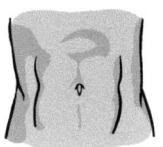

belly button

melic

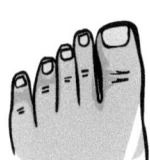

toe

dit gros del peu

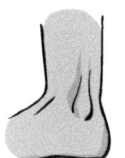

heel

taló

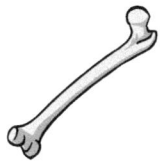

bone

os

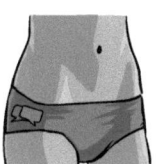

hip

maluc

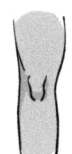

knee

genoll

elbow

colze

nose

nas

bottom

cul

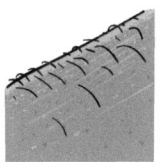

skin

pell

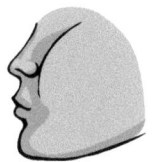

cheek

galta

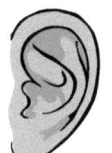

ear

orella

lip

llavi

mouth

boca

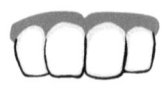

tooth

dent

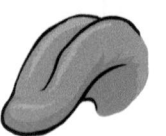

tongue

llengua

brain

cervell

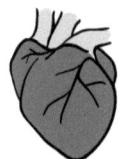

heart

cor

muscle

múscul

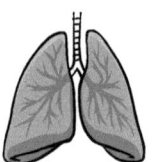

lung

pulmó

liver

fetge

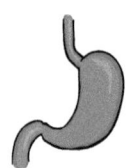

stomach

estómac

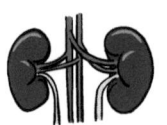

kidneys

ronyó

sex

relació sexual

condom

preservatiu

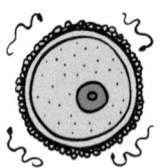

ovum

ovari

semen

semen

pregnancy

prenyat

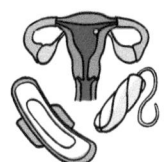

menstruation

menstruació

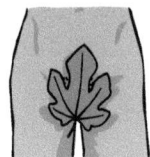

vagina

vagina

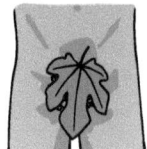

penis

penis

eyebrow

cella

hair

cabells

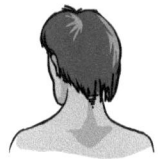

neck

coll

hospital

hospital

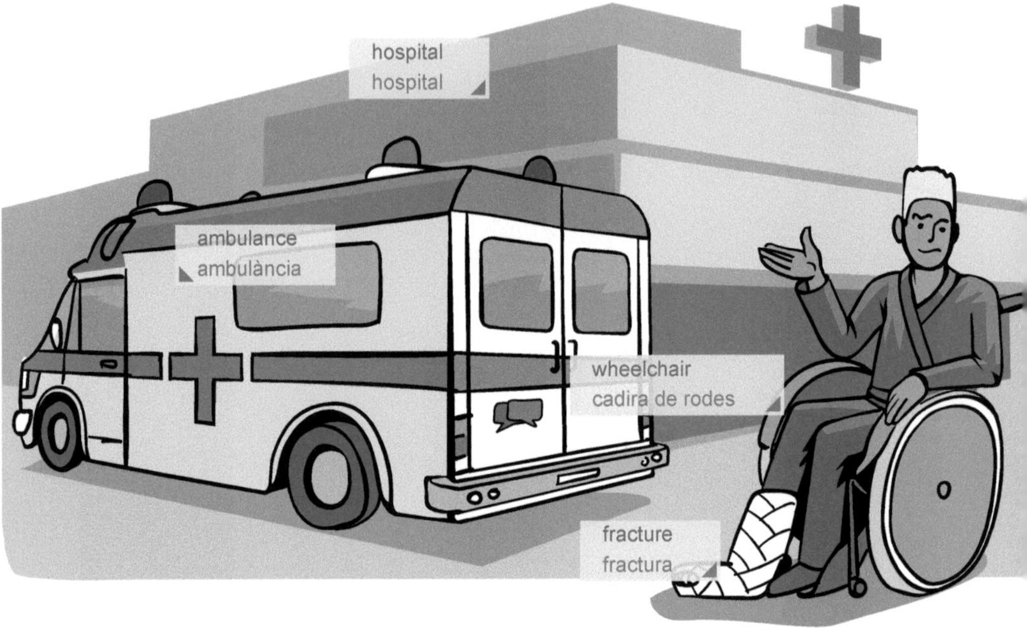

hospital
hospital
ambulance
ambulància
wheelchair
cadira de rodes
fracture
fractura

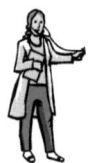

doctor
doctora

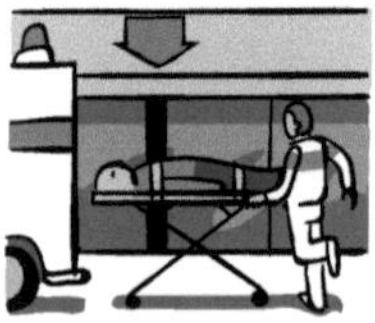

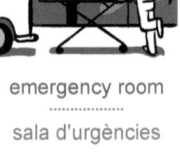

emergency room
sala d'urgències

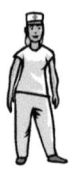

nurse
infermera

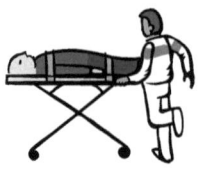

emergency
urgència

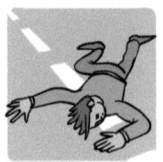

unconscious
inconscient

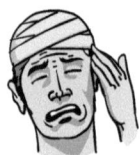

pain
dolor

injury

ferida

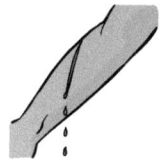

bleeding

sagnament

heart attack

atac de cor

stroke

apoplexia

allergy

al·lèrgia

cough

tos

fever

febre

flu

gripa

diarrhoea

diarrea

headache

mal de cap

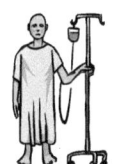

cancer

càncer

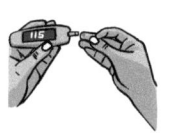

diabetes

diabetis

surgeon

cirurgià

scalpel

escalpel

operation

operació

CT

tomografia computada (TC), TAC

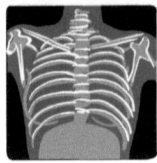

x-ray

raigs x

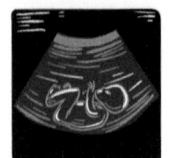

ultrasound

ultrasò

face mask

mascareta

disease

malaltia

waiting room

sala d'espera

crutch

crossa

plaster

tireta

bandage

embenat

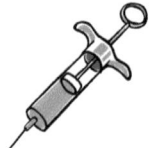

injection

injecció

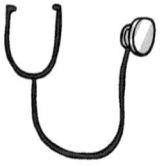

stethoscope

estetoscopi

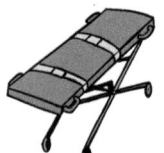

stretcher

llitera

clinical thermometer

termòmetre clínic

birth

pariment

overweight

sobrepès

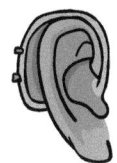

hearing aid

aparell auditiu

disinfectant

desinfectant

infection

infecció

virus

virus

HIV / AIDS

VIH / SIDA

medicine

medicina

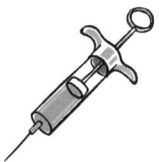

vaccination

vaccí

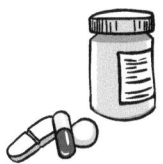

tablets

comprimits

pill

píl·lola

emergency call

trucada d'urgència

blood pressure monitor

tensiòmetre

ill / healthy

malalt / sà

Help!

Socors!

alarm

alarma

assault

assalt

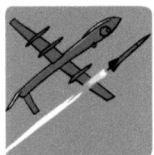

attack

atac

danger

perill

emergency exit

sortida-eixida d'urgència

Fire!

Foc!

fire extinguisher

extintor

accident

accident

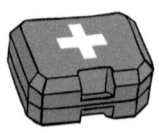

first-aid kit

farmaciola de primers
auxilis

SOS

SOS

police

policia

Europe

Europa

North America

Amèrica del Nord

South America

Amèrica del Sud

Africa

Àfrica

Asia

Àsia

Australia

Austràlia

Atlantic

Atlàntic

Pacific

Pacífic

Indian Ocean

Oceà Índic

Antarctic Ocean

Oceà Antàrtic

Arctic Ocean

Oceà Àrtic

North Pole

pol nord

South Pole

pol sud

Antarctica

Antàrtida

Earth

terra

land

país

sea

mar

island

illa

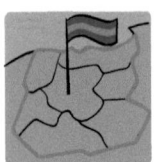

nation

nació

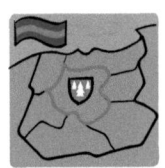

state

estat

clock face

quadrant

hour hand

agulla de les hores

minute hand

agulla dels minuts

second hand

agulla dels segons

What time is it?

Quina hora és?

day

dia

time

temps

now

ara

digital watch

rellotge digital

minute

minut

hour

hora

week

setmana

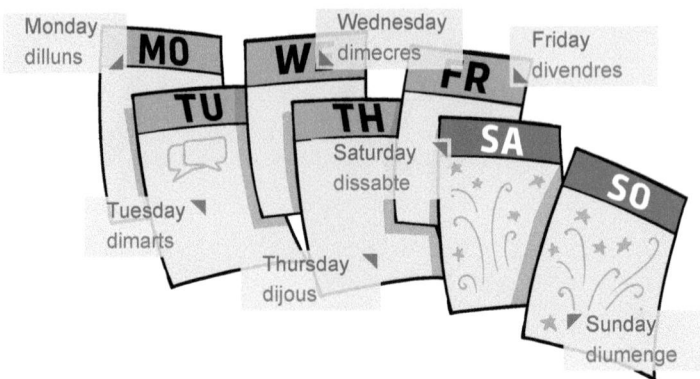

Monday dilluns

Tuesday dimarts

Wednesday dimecres

Thursday dijous

Friday divendres

Saturday dissabte

Sunday diumenge

yesterday

ahir

today

avui

tomorrow

demà

morning

matí

noon

migdia

evening

tarda

business days

dia feiner

weekend

cap de setmana

year

any

rain
pluja
rainbow
arc de Sant Martí
snow
neu
wind
vent
spring
primavera
autumn
tardor
summer
estiu
winter
hivern

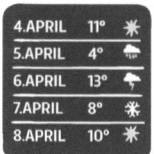

4.APRIL 11°
5.APRIL 4°
6.APRIL 13°
7.APRIL 8°
8.APRIL 10°

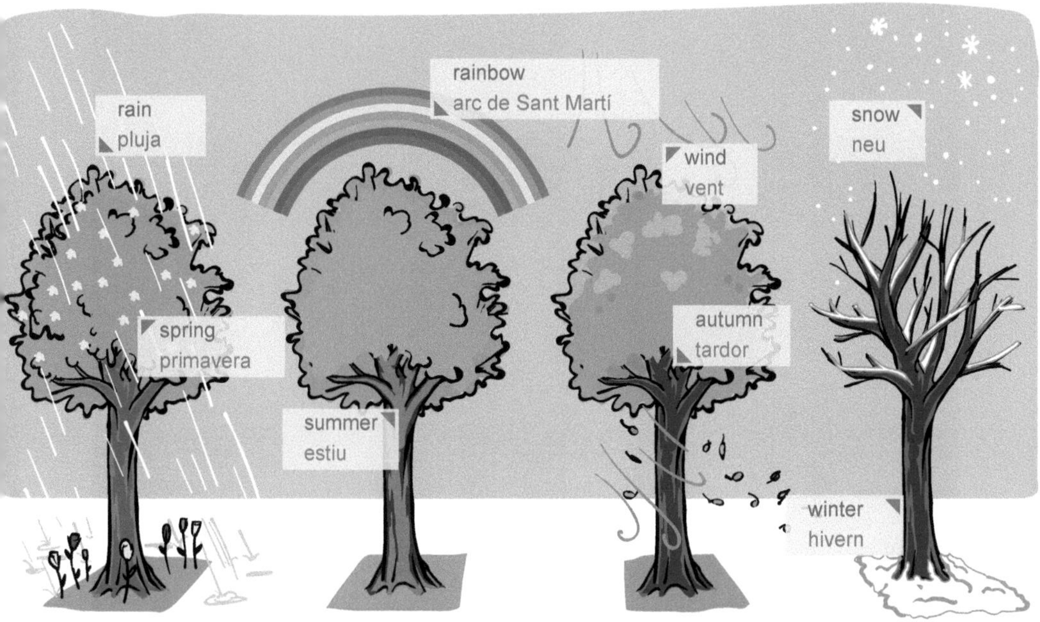

weather forecast

pronòstic del temps

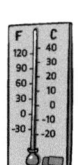

thermometer

termòmetre

sunshine

llum del sol

cloud

núvol

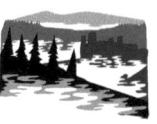

fog

boira

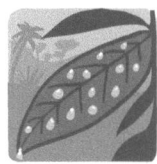

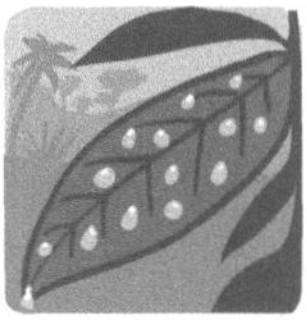

humidity

humiditat de l'aire

lightning

llamp

thunder

tro

storm

tempesta

hail

calamarsa

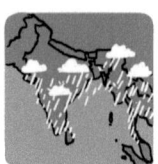

monsoon

monsó

flood

inundació

ice

gel

January

gener

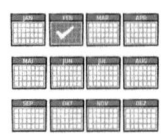

February

febrer

March

març

April

abril

May

maig

June

juny

July

juliol

August

agost

September
....
setembre

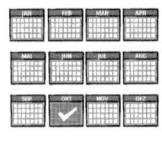

October
....
octubre

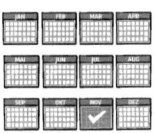

November
....
novembre

December
....
desembre

circle
....
cercle

square
....
quadrat

rectangle
....
rectangle

triangle
....
triangle

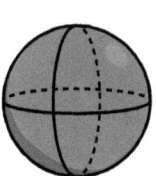

sphere
....
esfera

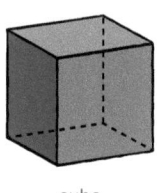

cube
....
cub

white

blanc

yellow

groc

orange

taronja

pink

rosa

red

vermell

purple

lila

blue

blau

green

verd

brown

marró

grey

gris

black

negre

a lot / a little

molt / poc

angry / calm

emprenyat / tranquil

beautiful / ugly

bonic / lleig

beginning / end

començament / fi

big / small

gran / petit

bright / dark

clar / fosc

brother / sister

germà / germana

clean / dirty

net / brut

complete / incomplete

complet / incomplet

day / night

dia / nit

dead / alive

mort / viu

wide / narrow

ample / estret

edible / inedible

comestible / immenjable

evil / kind

dolent / amable

excited / bored

entusiasmat / entediat

fat / thin

gros / prim

first / last

primer / darrer

friend / enemy

amic / enemic

full / empty

ple / buit

hard / soft

dur / tou

heavy / light

pesant / lleuger

hunger / thirst

gana / set

ill / healthy

malalt / sà

illegal / legal

il·legal / legal

intelligent / stupid

intel·ligent / ximple

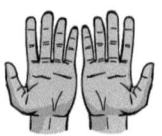

left / right

esquerra / dreta

near / far

prop / llunyà

new / used

nou / usat

nothing / something

res / quelcom

old / young

vell / jove

on / off

encès / apagat

open / closed

obert / tancat

quiet / loud

silenciós / sorollós

rich / poor

ric / pobre

right / wrong

correcte / incorrecte

rough / smooth

aspre / suau

sad / happy

trist / content

short / long

curt / llarg

slow / fast

lent / ràpid

wet / dry

humit / sec - eixut

warm / cool

calent / fred

war / peace

guerra / pau

0

zero

zero

1

one

u

2

two

dos

3

three

tres

4

four

quatre

5

five

cinc

6

six

sis

7

seven

set

8

eight

vuit

9

nine

nou

10

ten

deu

11

eleven

onze

12

twelve

dotze

13

thirteen

tretze

14

fourteen

catorze

15

fifteen

quinze

16

sixteen

setze

17

seventeen

disset

18

eighteen

divuit

19

nineteen

dinou

20

twenty

vint

100

hundred

cent

1.000

thousand

mil

1.000.000

million

milió

numbers - nombres

English
....
anglès

American English
....
anglès americà

Chinese Mandarin
....
xinès mandarí

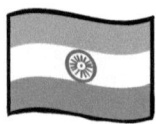

Hindi
....
hindi

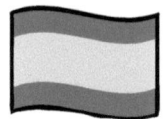

Spanish
....
espanyol

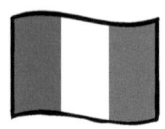

French
....
francès

Arabic
....
àrab

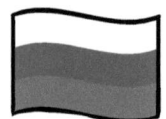

Russian
....
rus

Portuguese
....
portuguès

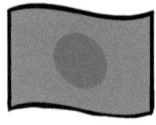

Bengali
....
bengalí

German
....
alemany

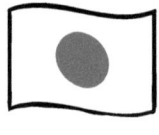

Japanese
....
japonès

I

jo

you

tu

he / she / it

ell / ella / allò

we

nosaltres

you

vosaltres

they

ells

who?

qui?

what?

què?

how?

com?

where?

on?

when?

quan?

name

nom

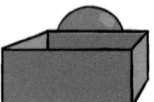

behind

darrere

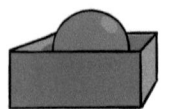

in

en

in front of

davant de

over

damunt

on

sobre

under

sota

beside

al costat

between

entre

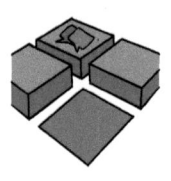

place

lloc